MW01711633

Fish Tales and Rainbow Colors:

POEMS FOR CHILDREN

by

Elizabeth A. Newton

Beth Newton

ISBN: 978-1-946977-85-4
Fish Tales and Rainbow Colors: Poems for Children

Yorkshire Publishing
3207 South Norwood Avenue
Tulsa, Oklahoma 74135
www.YorkshirePublishing.com
918.394.2665

This book is dedicated to my children, Bryan Hayes and Renee' Elizabeth Newton; also to my firstborn grandchild, Kian Michael.

Acknowledgements

My mother, Martha Roden Wilson, for believing in me through my writing journey; Frank Porter, for introducing me to Tate Publishing; Amanda Rodenbaugh, Whitehall Public Library; and to my great-grandfather John Francis Roden who wrote before me under the pen name of John Kelly.

KIAN
KIAN
KIAN

My Fish Tale

Last night I had the wildest dream.
I walked down to the lake.
I brought my worms and fishing pole
In pajamas for heaven's sake!

With worm on hook and pole in hand,
I sat down on the pier
And waited for a fish to bite.
I dreamt it took a year!

When all at once my line went taut,
And much to my surprise,
The biggest fish I'd ever seen.
I couldn't believe my eyes!

My big catch then began to grow
When I put him on the string.
I had to find a way right then
To wake up from this dream!

This is what I get I guess
For telling my fish tales.
They came to life in all my dreams,
From minnows into whales!

All Aboard

"Come along, we're moving out.
All aboard," the conductor shouts.
"Take your seats, sit right down.
This big train's going out of town!"

The engine roars, the whistle blows,
Her wheels are turning, there she goes!
Creaking, creaking along the track,
Through a tunnel, clickety-clack!

Up a hill, down a hill,
Up a hill again.
Rolling, speeding down the track,
All around the bend!

Over a bridge with thick black steam,
Her brakes are used, hear them scream.
The train slows down, the station in sight.
There's Grandpa waiting to hug me tight!

Fun at the Zoo

Who wants to take a trip to the zoo,
To see a monkey, a tiger, a kangaroo?
Hear the lions when they roar,
Watch the eagles as they soar.

Let's go find the big brown bears,
Who pace in their cage
While walking in pairs.

See the snakes, they slither and slide.
The prairie dogs, they love to hide.
The elephants are big and gray,
How they love their peanuts and hay.

Next come the turkeys, ducks, and hens,
Who gobble and quack
And squawk in their pens.

The swans are really a pretty sight,
Swimming and playing for all their might.
The goats and zebras are over there.
Animals, animals everywhere!

The elk, they stand so proud indeed
While buffalos begin to stampede.
There are pigs and chickens along the trail.
Let's take a look at that beautiful quail.
We can feed deer and llamas and little lambs too.
Don't forget the fluffy sheep
And ponies to ride for me and you.
What a great time we had at the zoo!

The Man in the Moon

The man in the moon became my friend
Many years ago
When I was just a little girl.
My grandma told me so.

She said he'd wink his eye at me
When the day turned into night,
Bringing down to earth his glow,
Peeking into sight.

So I looked up in the sky so dark
To greet my shining friend
Sitting high above the twinkling stars
In a space that never ends.

"Good evening, Mr. Moon," I'd say.
"How are you tonight?
Will you tell a story of the stars
And a comet in its flight?"
"Yes, my child, I surely will.
With your pretty face agleam,
Close your eyes and listen close,
I'll tell you in your dreams."

RED
ORANGE
YELLOW
GREEN
BLUE
INDIGO
VIOLET

Colors of the Rainbow

The rainbow hides the clouds away
On a gloomy afternoon.
She lingers there beneath the sun
On a rainy day in June.

The misty skies begin to clear
As she peeks up over the hill,
Showing off her colors there,
Shining as she will.

Now each color has a meaning.
I'll explain them one by one,
Displaying all her brilliance
Under the golden sun.

The green is for the grass to grow
After the rain has fallen.
The blue is for the sky above
To clear for angels calling.

The indigo and violet are for
The shadows in the night.
The yellow is the moon that glows,
Showing off her light.

Red is the flaming color
That stands out most of all,
But the orange stands for the big round sun
The rainbow loves to call.

Are There Really Angels?

Have you ever seen an angel?
Was she really all in white?
Did she play a harp?
Did she play a trumpet?
Did you see her in the night?

Does an angel really have wings?
Or is it all a story?
Does she talk with us when we pray,
A messenger of God's glory?

I know for sure there is a heaven,
And I pray to God above.
So there must be lots of angels,
Who can doubt their love?

Sing, Mountains, Sing

The mountains here are picturesque
With snow upon their peaks.
They seem so noble standing there,
Yet being soft and meek.

The wind, it whistles through its trees
From a distant tier below,
Sending a message down its slope,
"I'm calling for the snow."

All along the mountainside
This message can be heard.
It's passed on to the little child,
Who passes on the word,

"Winter will be on its way.
I know it to be true.
I've heard it from the mountains.
Oh, what a lovely view."

Even a whisper in time can be heard
From a mountaintop each day,
Saying, "Come to me,
Bring your skis,
Enjoy this wonderful day!"

Winter Fun

Glistening snow upon the trees
And cold winds blowing by,
Lets us know that winter's here,
Its beauty wins a prize.

Bundle up with boots and hat,
Scarf and mittens too.
Crunch the snow beneath your feet,
Play as children do.

Make a snowman, build a fort,
Have a gay ole time,
Throwing snowballs one by one
Behind the enemy line!

Angels are also fun to make
With our hands and feet.
Just lie down in the deep, deep snow,
Impressions it will keep.

Winter is never boring.
There're always things to do.
As long as we think like children,
We can play their fun games too!

Mail, Mail, Mail

Don't you wish you'd get some mail
Like Mommy and Daddy do.
In so many sizes, colors, and shapes,
In boxes and cartons too.

There are pretty stamps of blue and red
That we can buy today,
To place upon the envelope
And send it on its way.

Send it first, second, or third class now.
The difference is the time it takes
To send it to one's house.
If you send your mail as certified,
It costs a little more.
But you're guaranteed they'll get it,
A receipt for you to show for.

Birthday cards, Christmas cards,
St. Patrick and Valentines too,
Are all the nicest things to see
In the mailbox just for you.

Mail is meant for everyone,
Of any size or age.
We send it and receive it,
Reading through every page.

CPSIA information can be obtained
at www.ICGtesting.com
Printed in the USA
BVOW10s0653200717
489653BV00009B/44/P

9 781946 977854